P9-DIA-271

AMAZING ASIAN AMERICANS

Amazing Asian Americans

Yo-Yo and Yeou-Cheng Ma,
Finding Their Way

by
Ai-Ling Louie

Illustrated by
Cathy Peng

Yo-Yo and Yeou-Cheng Ma, Finding Their Way: Amazing Asian Americans

To Melanie and Wesley—A.L.
For Audrey, my sister.—C.P.

Copyright ©2012 by Ai-Ling Louie. All rights reserved. No part of this publication may be reproduced, stored in a retrieval system or transmitted in any form or by any means, electronic, mechanical, photocopying, recording or otherwise without the prior written permission of the copyright holder, except brief quotations used in a review.

Illustrations © 2012 by Cathy Peng

Designed by Jonathan Louie
Printed on 115gsm US comic woodfree
ISBN-978-0-978746506
Library of Congress Control Number: 2011946170
Published by
Dragoneagle Press
Box 30856
Bethesda, MD 20824 U.S.A.
Dragoneagle.com

Published 2012
First paperback printing March 2012

Publisher's Cataloging-in-Publication Data
Louie, Ai-Ling. 1949-
    Yo-Yo and Yeou-Cheng Ma, Finding Their Way: Amazing Asian Americans/ by Ai-Ling Louie
    Illustrations by Cathy Peng
    Series: Amazing Asian Americans
    Summary. A biography of the cellist Yo-Yo Ma and his sister Yeou-Cheng, who started out wanting to be a violinist but left her musical studies to become a physician.
    Includes notes, timeline, children's bibliography, discography, selected references.
    ISBN – 978-0-978746506
    1. Ma, Yeou-Cheng. 1951- —Juvenile Literature
    2. Ma, Yo-Yo. 1955- —Juvenile Literature
    3. Musicians—United States—Biography—Juvenile Literature
    4. Cellists—United States—Biography—Juvenile Literature
    5. Chinese Americans—Biography—Juvenile Literature
    I. Peng, Cathy. 1975- ill.

2012
787.3

Manufactured in Hong Kong by Regal Printing Limited
Photo Credits: back top flap, Jonathan Louie; bottom, Matthew Bennett. Page 48 iStock

AMAZING ASIAN AMERICANS

Yo-Yo
and
Yeou-Cheng Ma
Finding Their Way

Amazing Asian Americans

by Ai-Ling Louie

illustrated by Cathy Peng

dragoneagle press

In a small apartment in the city of Paris in the country called France, Yeou-Cheng Ma was learning the violin. She was only four years old but her father had already been teaching her for over a year. Ba Ba played some notes on his own violin. Then he said, "That is the next part of the piece. You will practice it all week. Then you can add it to the part you already know. Soon you'll know the whole piece of music. Now go and play for one half hour. I'll tell you when you can stop."

In this way, Yeou-Chéng had already learned
several long pieces of music. She could play them by heart.
She thought all children learned the violin this way. She
didn't know that she was the first child to learn by her
father's method. He was a doctor of Musicology. Dr. Ma
believed that using his method children did not have to
wait until they were 7 or 8 to learn music.

With Yeou-Cheng practicing, Dr. Ma turned to
his son. Yo-Yo' was only 7 months old. Ba Ba pressed a
toy violin into his son's hands.
He cupped the baby's left hand over the strings.

"Yo-Yo is too young to play the violin,"
Yeou-Cheng said to her mother.

When it came to the children's music
education, Marina Ma usually gave her husband
his way. She might be living in Paris, but
she was still a Chinese woman
who believed in the old
Chinese way. "We all must
do as Ba Ba says," she
told Yeou-Cheng. "He is
the head of our
household."

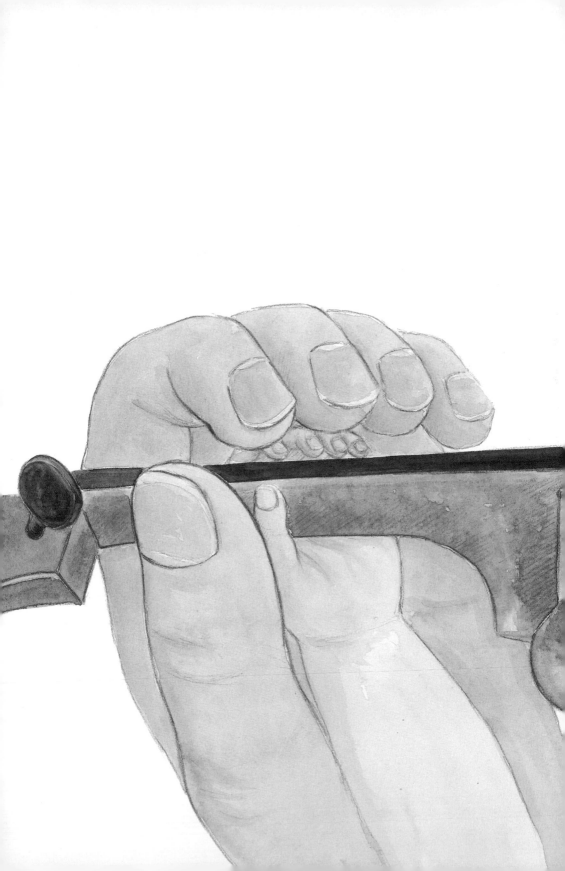

Yeou-Cheng practiced every day. But when her father led her up to the stage at her first violin competition, she was afraid. "You can do it," her father whispered to her. "Play it just as you've practiced at home."

Yeou-Cheng, looked out at the audience. Everyone was staring at her. Sitting in the first row she saw all the teenagers who had played before her. How could she ever beat them? Ma Ma nodded and smiled from the audience. Yeou-Cheng picked up her bow and put it to the strings. Once she started playing it was easy. She knew the piece so well she didn't have to think about it.

At the end of the competition an announcer came to the stage. "And the winner is… Yeou-Cheng Ma!" Ma Ma threw her arms around Yeou-Cheng. "I'm so proud of you!" she told her. Yeou-Cheng looked over at her father. Men were all around him patting him on

the back. All because of her. Winning music competitions made little Yeou-Cheng happy, especially because it pleased her parents. One day she would grow up to be a fine musician, just like Ba Ba said.

Her little brother Yo-Yo did not share Yeou-Cheng's serious personality. When he was three years old Ba Ba gave Yo-Yo his sister's old violin. "Look what I've got for you!" Ba Ba said.

Yo-Yo hopped around the apartment. He sang a little song about a frog. "Yo Yo, this is important!" Ba Ba said. Yo-Yo kept singing and hopping around. Dr. Ma waved the violin and said, "Come here!" Yo-Yo hopped farther away from his father. Finally Ba Ba caught Yo-Yo and set him down in front of him. He put

his left hand on the strings and showed him where to press down to play a D. "Now draw your bow across to make the sound." Yo-Yo did as his father said.

"Can I go now?"

"No, you cannot! Practice what I've showed you. I'll tell you when you are finished."

Yo-Yo sighed. He did not want to practice.

"Oh, dear!" Ma Ma said.

Yeou-Cheng nodded. Her little brother was not a musician like she was.

"I hate the
violin!" Yo-Yo said a few days
later when he and his sister were in the park.

"Why?" asked Yeou-Cheng. "Ba Ba plays the
violin and I play the violin."

"That's right—it's YOUR instrument!" Yo-Yo said.
Then he ran far away.

A few days later, when
Yo-Yo was alone with
his violin it somehow got
broken. It looked like there
would only be one young
musician in the Ma family.

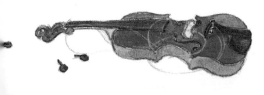

Although Ba Ba taught Yeou-Cheng classical
Western music like Bach, Mozart and other European
composers of the 1600s and 1700s, he liked all sorts of
music. One night the family went to a jazz concert at
the University. Jazz music was from America. It was
more modern. In the jazz band there was a trumpet,
a clarinet, a piano, a drummer, and a double bass[2]. The
man who played the double bass plucked the strings
with his right hand.

Yo-Yo jumped up in his seat. He pointed at the
double bass. "I want that!" he declared. "I want to play
the big instrument"[3]. The double bass was twice the size
of little Yo-Yo. But he was a very stubborn child.

So a few days later Dr. Ma brought home a cello. A cello is smaller than the double bass Yo-Yo wanted, but it was much bigger than a violin. It was so big it had to be played sitting down. Yo-Yo's face lit up when he saw it. For the first time in his life he was excited about playing music.

Yeou-Cheng was glad her brother had his own instrument to play. Now they could practice together. Even if he wasn't going to be a fine musician like Yeou-Cheng would be one day. Ba Ba even started her on a second instrument: the piano.

With all the practicing they had to do, plus learning French, Chinese and math at home, the Ma children had no time for friends or playmates. But they had each other.

Yo-Yo came to all his sister's recitals. After one concert Yeou-Cheng ran off the stage and sat down next to her brother. "How was I?" she asked.

"Good!" he told her.

"Just good?" she teased. "Is that all you have to say?"

"Well… your sound is a little off."

"What?" she said. "What do you mean?"

"You were just a little," Yo-Yo said.

Yeou-Cheng didn't like what Yo-Yo was telling her. But when she looked to her father for help he said, "Yo-Yo is right." He looked curiously at his son. "He has a very good ear."

Soon Yo-Yo himself was ready to play his cello on stage at the University. Yeou-Cheng would accompany him on the piano.

She helped her brother tie his bowtie. She combed his hair. "Don't be nervous. Think of how nice it will be when it's all over—that's what I do. You only have to play a little portion of your piece. It won't take long."

Yo-Yo called to Ba Ba. "I'm going to play the whole piece," he told him.

"What?" said Dr. Ma. No one in the family ever told him what to do, especially not a six-year-old! "You do as I planned," Dr. Ma said.

Yo-Yo said, "This is what I'll do: I'll play the first part and everybody will clap loudly. You clap loudly too. That will mean they want to hear more. So, I'll sit down and play the rest."

Dr. Ma wasn't sure, but everything worked just as the boy said. He played the whole piece to thunderous applause.

Dr. Ma had a brother who lived in the United States. When Yeou-Cheng was 11, in 1962, the family went to visit him and his family. Word got out that the Ma family of Rochester, New York had very talented children visiting them. Yeou-Cheng and Yo-Yo played at a concert in Rochester and then in Denver.

And then something incredible happened—the Ma children were invited to play in front of John F. Kennedy, the President of the United States in Washington, DC, the Capital!

The Washington Armory seated 5,000. When Yeou-Cheng saw the huge crowd she was more than a little scared. Yo-Yo was looking nervous too. "What's the matter?" Ba Ba said. "You're usually not like this."

"It's just that my cello is so small and this place is so big."[4]

Ba Ba laughed. "Don't worry! The loudspeakers will make sure everyone can hear you."

The concert was exciting. Yeou-Cheng played her piece perfectly. The next day the concert was even written up in the newspapers. There were many pictures of Yo-Yo with his cello. But not a single picture of Yeou-Cheng. She scoured all the articles and never even found her name.

Dr. Ma liked everything he saw about America. His methods of training his children were praised as revolutionary. He was even offered a job in New York City teaching music at the Trent School for children. They wanted him to start a children's orchestra. It was decided: The Ma family was moving to New York.

In New York, Yeou-Cheng and Yo-Yo went to school for the first time. And the school was in English, a language neither of them knew. Sometimes in class Yeou-Cheng knew the answer to the teacher's questions but could only think of the word in French or Chinese. "Yeou-Cheng," her teacher called one afternoon when the class was studying history, "what did you think about the French and Indian War?"

Yeou-Cheng did not know what to say in English, French or Chinese. She was not used to being asked what she thought about anything. It was a relief for Yeou-Cheng to leave school at the end of the day and go to her music lesson. She knew she was good at violin. She didn't need anything else. She was going to be a fine musician, just as Ba Ba had told her when she was a little girl. She and Yo-Yo both had new teachers in America. Yo-Yo was studying with a well-known cellist, Janos Schulz. When he heard Yo-Yo play he offered to teach the child prodigy[5] for free.

But one day when Yeou-Cheng got to her violin lesson her teacher had bad news. "This will be our last lesson," he said. "Didn't your parents tell you?"

Yeou-Cheng stared at him in shock. "Why?" she asked.

"I told your parents I think you should stick to piano," he said. "You play the notes perfectly on the violin, but you don't make the notes sing. On the piano, you'll be able to help your brother when he needs somebody to play duets."

Yeou-Cheng ran out of the lesson. Accompany her brother on duets! Was that all she was good for? She didn't want to believe it, but deep down she knew it was true. She could hear how fast Yo-Yo progressed on the cello. She heard people who knew music praise the way he played. Most of all, she heard the beauty of the music. He made the notes sing.

Yeou-Cheng would never be the musician that she dreamed of being. But if she weren't a musician what would she be? She thought of her teacher's words in school again: "What do you think, Yeou-Cheng?" Her friends at school were planning to go to college. When they asked Yeou-Cheng what she was going to do after high school, she just shrugged.

One afternoon Yeou-Cheng sat in Chemistry class. Her teacher was handing back the latest test. "And with a perfect score again—Yeou-Cheng. Congratulations!" She dropped the test paper on Yeou-Cheng's desk.

Yeou-Cheng had top grades in Biology, Physics, and Math too. She really enjoyed those subjects. But she had never thought they could be her life. Her life was Music. Now her life could be anything she wanted it to be. Yeou-Cheng applied to college and went to Harvard University in Cambridge, Massachusetts. For the first time in her life she lived away from her family and away from her talented brother. That was just fine with her.

Yeou-Cheng threw herself into college life. She made friends. She loved living in the girls' dorm, and studying Chemistry and Biology. All the training she had as a child learning music, French, Chinese and English made studying easy.

"I want to be a doctor," she told her parents. "I want to help people get well. After I graduate, I want to go to Harvard Medical School."

"Only the best students get in there," Dr. Ma told her.

"Yeou-Cheng is the best!" Yo-Yo said.

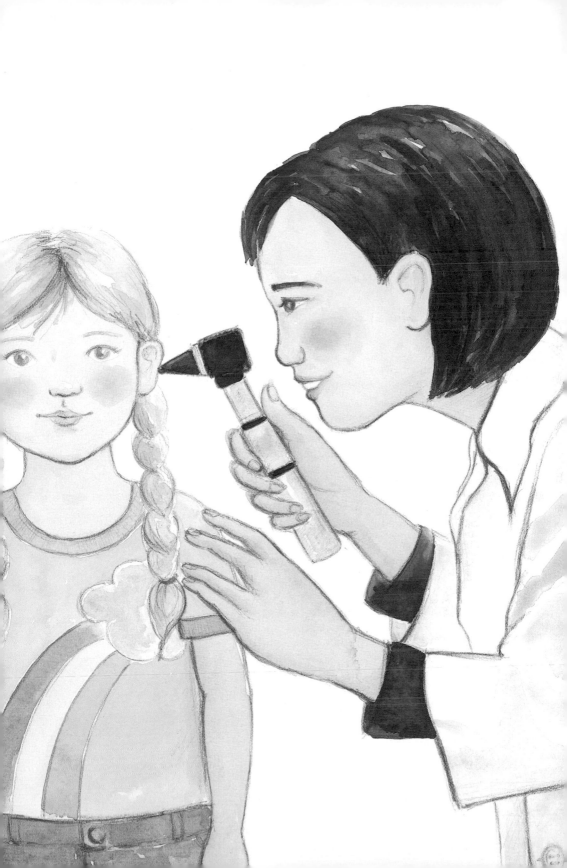

Yo-Yo was fifteen now. He
was a student at Juilliard, a famous
music school in New York. He still played in his father's
orchestra. But when it came time to apply to college
Yo-Yo wanted to follow his sister's path to Harvard.

"Juilliard is the best musical training you can
have," Ba Ba said one night.

"My life has always been musical training,"
Yo-Yo said. "It's lonely and boring. I don't want to
practice all the time."

Ma Ma sighed.
Ba Ba and Yo-Yo were
always arguing. Ba Ba
was the head of their
household. But this
time Yo-Yo was not
backing down.

"Look," he
said finally. "If you
want me to be really obedient,
I can do that, but that means never
finding my own voice. If you want me to be a good
musician, it means I have to find myself."[6]

Dr. Ma thought long and hard about what his son
said. It was hard to let him do something he thought
was wrong. But his son was growing up.

SAN
tribal mask

Yo-Yo took things into his own hands. He enrolled in Harvard and moved to Cambridge. He studied African culture and Sociology, the study of people and how they live together. He had a girlfriend, Jill Hornor, and made lots of new friends.

He was right there in the audience when
Yeou-Cheng received her degree from Harvard Medical
School. She already knew what kind of doctor she
wanted to be—a pediatrician, a doctor who helps
children. She went on to work at the Albert Einstein
Medical Center in Bronx, New York. She specialized
in the development of children's hearing. She, along with
her husband, musician Michael Dadap, also
restarted her father's Children's
Orchestra Society.

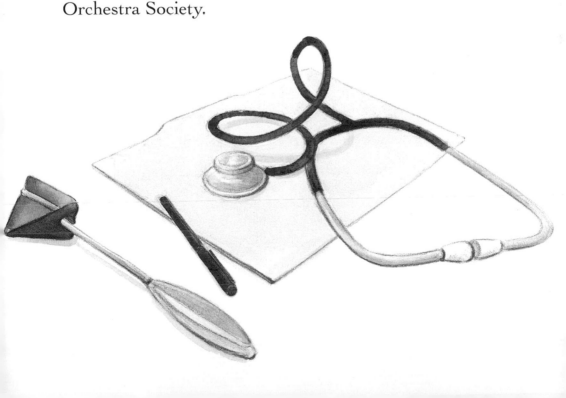

Sometimes they take the children
in the orchestra to Carnegie Hall, the
concert hall in New York, to hear the
world famous musician, her brother
Yo-Yo Ma.

Yo-Yo travels all over the world
giving concerts. He has recorded 78 CD's and
won the top award in music, the Grammy, 15 times.
Yo-Yo still loves to make new friends: he has played
with Argentine tango players, and Appalachian fiddlers.
Recently he created The Silk Road[7] project. He brought
together musicians from all along the ancient trade route
to play together—players of the Chinese pipa[8], Iranian
kemancheh[9], and Indian tabla[10]. Yo-Yo, the
Chinese, French, American, sees himself as a
citizen of the world and believes music to
be the universal language.

In 2008 Yo-Yo was invited to play at the Inauguration of another U.S. President, Barack Obama. It was an exciting day, but he had even more fun when he played as a surprise guest at the Children's Orchestra Society concert. He played alongside his sister, Yeou-Cheng.

They will always have each other.

Notes

1. Yo-Yo's name in Chinese is written 友友. Friendly is written twice, emphasizing his friendliness. Yeou-Cheng (pronounced Yo Cheng) 友乘 shares the same first character with her brother, and the second one means multiplied, meaning she has lots of friends. (Yeou-Cheng's name courtesy of correspondence between the author and Yeou-Cheng Ma, 1/7/2011)

2. Bass, pronounced base

3. Ma, Marina. (1995) My Son, Yo-Yo, p. 29

4. Ibid., p.82.

5. Ibid., p. 130. Prodigy is pronounced PROD-ĭ-jee. A child prodigy is someone who is extremely advanced for his age in an art or subject. Some become very famous as adults. Mozart was composing at age five and then went on to become one of the most beloved composers of all time. Other child prodigies are never heard from as adults.

6. Hirshey, Gerri. (2005) "We Are the World, Cellist Yo-Yo Ma" Parade Magazine, January 30.

7. The Silk Road existed from the 600s B.C. to the early 1900s A.D. . Silk, spices, books, and more were carried on camels.

8. The pipa is a short-necked wooden lute that is plucked.

9. The kemancheh is a small, round-bodied fiddle with a spike at its base.

10. The tabla is a pair of small drums.

Selected Discography and Videography

Ma, Yo-Yo and others (1997) *Soul of the Tango; the Music of Astor Piazolla* (Audio CD) New York: Sony.

Ma, Yo-Yo and others (2000) *Appalachian Journey* (Audio CD) New York: Sony.

Ma, Yo-Yo and others (2002) *Silk Road Journeys* (Audio CD) New York: Sony.

Ma, Yo-Yo and others (2005) *Yo-Yo Ma, the Complete Cello Suites: Inspired by Bach.* (DVD set) New York: Sony.

Ma, Yo-Yo (2005) *The Essential Yo-Yo Ma* (Audio CD) New York: Sony.

Ma, Yo-Yo (2006) *J.S. Bach: the 6 Unaccompanied Cello Suites* ((Audio CD) New York: Sony

Bibliography of Children's Materials

Ceceri, Kathryn. (2011) *The Silk Road: 20 Projects Explore the World's Most Famous Trade Route (Build It Yourself)*. White River Junction, VT: Nomad Press.

Chippendale, Lisa. (2004) *Yo-Yo Ma: A Cello Superstar Brings Music to the World*. Berkeley Heights, NJ: Enslow.

Demi. (2008) *Marco Polo*. Tarrytown, NY: Marshall Cavendish.

Gilchrist, Cherry. (2005) *Stories from the Silk Road*. Barefoot Books, Cambridge, MA.

Krebs, Laurie and Cann, Helen. (2005) *We're Riding on a Caravan, An Adventure on the Silk Road*. Cambridge, MA: Barefoot Books.

Major, John S. (2002) *Caravan to America, Living Arts of the Silk Road*. Cricket Books, Chicago, IL.

Nathan, Amy. (2006) *Meet the Musicians: From Prodigies (or not) to Pros*. New York: Henry Holt.

(2002) *The Silk Road*, Calliope Magazine. February 2002, Vol. 12, #6, pps. 1-49

Sis, Peter. (2006) *Play Mozart Play*. New York: Greenwillow.

Selected References

Garfinkel, Jennifer. (2005) "Yo-Yo Ma's Sister Tells of the Healing Power of Music" *The Dartmouth,* February 3.

Gay, Peter. (1999) *Mozart,* New York: Lipper/Viking.

Gordon, Stewart. (2008) *The Silk Road, When Asia Was the World.* Cambridge, MA: Da Capo Press.

Hirshey, Gerri. (2005) "We Are the World (Cellist Yo-Yo Ma)" *Parade Magazine,* January 30.

Ma, Marina. (1995) *My Son, Yo-Yo.* Hong Kong: The Chinese University Press.

Manegold, Catherine S. (1994) "The Hidden Melody: At Home with Yeou-Cheng Ma." New York: *The New York Times,* March 10.

Tommasini, Anthony (1998) "That Children May Discover the Joy of Music: Rejecting a Concert Career, A Daughter Found Happiness in Her Father's Musical Vision." New York, *The New York Times.* May, 11.

Tassel, Janet. (2000) "Yo-Yo Ma's Journeys." Cambridge, MA: *Harvard Magazine,* March/April.

Thubron, Colin. (2007) *Shadow of the Silk Road.* New York: Harper.

http://www.yo-yoma.com, the official Yo-Yo Ma site.

http://www.childrensorch.org, the official website of the Children's Orchestra Society

Timeline

1951	Yeou-Cheng Ma born, July 28, Paris, France.
1955	Yo-Yo Ma born, October 7, Paris, France.
1961	Yo-Yo's first recital, Université de Paris, France.
1962	Yeou-Cheng and Yo-Yo Ma are performers at the Gala Benefit Concert, Washington Armory, November 29, Washington, DC.
1962–64	Yo-Yo studies with Janos Schulz, New York, NY.
1970–71	Yo-Yo attends Julliard's College Division.
1976	Yo-Yo graduates from Harvard College, Cambridge, MA.
1977	Yo-Yo marries Jill Hornor.
1977	Yeou-Cheng graduates from Harvard Medical School, Cambridge, MA.
1978	Yo-Yo wins the Avery Fisher Award for Classical Musician of Outstanding Achievement.
1979	Yo-Yo Ma's first recording, plays Finzi, *Concerto for Cello and Orchestra Op. 40* with London's Royal Philharmonic.
1984	Children's Orchestra Society revived by Yeou-Cheng and Michael Dadap. Queens, NY.
1986	Yo-Yo Ma's first Grammy Award for: Ma, Y., et al. (1986) *Brahms: Cello and Piano Sonatas in E Minor Op. 38, and F Op.99.* New York, RCA.
2002	Winter Olympics. February 8, Yo-Yo plays with Sting and the Mormon Tabernacle Choir at the Opening Ceremony, Salt Lake City, UT.
2008	Yo-Yo plays with Emanuel Ax, Gabriela Montero, and Anthony McGill at the Inauguration of President Obama, January 20, Washington, DC.
2011	Yo-Yo is awarded the Presidential Medal of Freedom and Kennedy Center Honors Medal.

AMAZING ASIAN AMERICANS

Amazing Asian Americans,
a series for the elementary school child.

Books in this series:
Vera Wang, Queen of Fashion

Yo-Yo and Yeou-Cheng Ma, Finding Their Way

To purchase copies visit our website:
dragoneagle.com

Coming next:
Jeremy Lin, No Slam Dunk
an ebook